THOUGHTS* FROM A MIND THAT NEVER RESTS

*AS WELL AS SOME AFTERTHOUGHTS WHILE AT REST

THOUGHTS* FROM A MIND THAT NEVER RESTS

*AS WELL AS SOME AFTERTHOUGHTS WHILE AT REST

by

KEN HANNA

ABOUT THE BOOK

This little book of thoughts and quotes has been put together to give <u>everyone</u> a chance to feel good about <u>something</u> in life. It was created out of the mind of its author with a format that would allow the reader to select any area of life that would need redirection, rethinking, remotivation, or just rereading.

This book should serve for lifetimes to come because the messages are eternally clear, simple, and to-the-point. There is nothing "deep" or confusing or hard to understand—they are simply there to grasp.

Your author is <u>positive</u> you will gain from it because it is <u>positive</u> in its direction. All you have to do is follow directions. Just enjoy all of the messages, and live your life on the "up" side (and never look "down")!

DEDICATION

This is <u>only</u> for my students (past/present/future), my family and friends, all I have ever known, and all I have never known. This is dedicated to everyone.) . . .

TABLE OF CONTENTS

INTRODUCTION

This little book contains some big thoughts! I hope the words have lasting meaning because all the meanings should last. My purpose in doing this was an outgrowth of my desire to convey simple solutions to many of the complex problems inherent with living. Also, I periodically find my brain in "overdrive"; at least, that is where it goes on its own on occasion.

If any of these thoughts "ring" familiar with your own thoughts or to any you may have heard, then I suspect our minds are in synch. "Feels good, doesn't it?"

Enjoy! And live a happy, peaceful life! Every moment, of a life of undetermined length, should be lived to its fullest and without an ounce of harm to anyone.

\

L

I

F

E

IF THERE WAS AN ALTERNATIVE TO LIVING,

CAN YOU IMAGINE WHAT THAT WOULD BE LIKE?

LIFE IS WHAT WE CALL

WHAT

WE DO!

LIFE ALLOWS US TO EXIST

       HERE AND NOW

IN PREPARATION FOR

       THERE AND THEN.

HOW WE LIVE WHILE WE ARE HERE

WILL HELP DETERMINE

OUR ETERNITY.

LIVE WITH THE KNOWLEDGE THAT

YOU WILL BE REMEMBERED

FOR BOTH THE GOOD AND BAD

THAT YOU DID;

YOU MUST DECIDE WHICH IS

MORE IMPORTANT!

WHAT WE DO WITH OUR LIVES

IS DETERMINED BY

WHAT WE DO IN OUR LIVES.

IF WE KNOW LIFE IS FINITE

AND WE ASSUME DEATH IS NOT,

WHY DO WE ALL WASTE

SO MUCH OF OUR TIME?

IF OUR LIVES ARE TO BE LIVED

      ETERNALLY IN HEAVEN,

WHAT DO THOSE IN HEAVEN

      CALL THIS?

THE TROUBLE WITH LIFE IS

WE HAVE TO LIVE IT!

TO LIVE A LIFE WITH NO POSITIVE REWARD,

IS TO HAVE NEVER LIVED YOUR LIFE!

TO ALLOW ANOTHER TO BEND

YOUR THOUGHTS,

IS TO ALLOW ANOTHER TO LIVE

YOUR LIFE!

TRY THAT WHICH WILL CHALLENGE YOU,

ELSE YOUR LIFE BE LIVED IN TOTAL

BOREDOM!

IF YOU ARE YOU,

        AS IT SHOULD BE,

YOU CAN BE

        NO ONE ELSE.

OUR BELIEF IN WHAT IS TO COME AFTER LIFE

HELPS US DETERMINE HOW WE APPROACH LIFE.

WHY NOT <u>LIVE</u> WITH THE INTENT

THAT YOU WILL AFTER DEATH?

IF YOU CAN PRETEND TO BE HAPPY

LONG ENOUGH,

YOU WILL BE!

THE BLEMISHES WE FACE IN LIFE

SHOULD BE TREATED WITH THE

CREAM OF CONSCIENCE.

HOW WE CONFRONT AND FACE OUR

DILEMMAS

IS HOW WE CAN TRULY JUDGE OUR WORTH.

OUR MOMENT OF TIME HERE

SHOULD BE SPENT

PREPARING FOR OUR TIME

YET TO BE SPENT.

SINCE WE DON'T KNOW WHAT IS ON

    THE OTHER SIDE, ·

SHOULD WE NOT MAKE THE MOST OF

    WHAT WE HAVE ON THIS SIDE?

LIFE GOES ON AND ON AND. . . . .

WE'RE JUST NOT ALLOWED

TO STICK AROUND AND WATCH.

D

E

A

T

H

23

IN ORDER TO GUARANTEE LIFE,

DEATH MUST EXIST.

THE ONLY THING DEATH DOES

IS

TAKE

AWAY

OUR ABILITY TO COMMUNICATE

DIRECTLY.

THE DEATH OF SOMEONE WE KNEW

ENHANCES OUR FEELINGS

ABOUT THAT PERSON.

DEATH

AS THE NEXT STAGE OF LIFE,

      WILL ANSWER QUESTIONS

WE NEED NOT BE IN A HURRY TO ASK.

DEATH WAS "CREATED"

SO YOU MIGHT BETTER APPRECIATE LIVING. . . . .

SO WHY DON'T YOU?

DEATH SIMPLY ERASES

THE PHYSICAL PRESENCE!

DEATH

IS THE

ULTIMATE CHANGE

IN

LIFE!

DEATH WAS "DESIGNED"

TO

MAKE

ROOM

FOR NEW THOUGHT!

WHEN YOUR DAYS ARE DONE

AND YOU ARE GONE,

LEAVE A MEMORY THAT WILL

JOYOUSLY LIVE ON.

NONE OF US IS HERE JUST TO BE FORGOTTEN;

SO LIVE AS NEED BE TO INSURE

ETERNAL MEMORY!

DEATH

IS NOTHING MORE THAN

ANOTHER FORM OF

LIFE!

THE FEAR OF DYING IS NOTHING MORE THAN

APPREHENSION

OF A JOURNEY WITH AN UNKNOWN

DESTINATION.

THE REALITY OF DEATH IS

THAT

IT

IS

COMPLETELY UNKNOWN TO US.

C
H
A
N
G
E

CHANGE IS BUT A CHANCE WE TAKE

BY SUBSTITUTING ONE LETTER.

IF MOST COULD CHANGE BUT ONE PART OF LIFE,

IT LIKELY WOULD BE DEATH.

IF MOST COULD CHANGE BUT ONE PART OF DEATH,

IT LIKELY WOULD BE LIFE.

WHAT HAS BEEN GAINED WHEN WHAT WE DO

HURTS SOMEONE ELSE?

IF YOU EVER FOUND PLEASURE IN

SOMEONE ELSE'S PAIN,

IMAGINE HOW MUCH PAIN YOU MUST HAVE HAD.

TO JOY IN SOMEONE'S FRAILTY

IS TO

REALLY DISLIKE YOURSELF!

ACCEPT THE OTHER PERSON FOR WHOM

THE PERSON IS,

NOT FOR WHOM YOU WANT THE PERSON TO BE.

CHANGE IS VERY OFTEN TRAUMATIC,

BUT ONLY BECAUSE WE ALLOW IT TO BE.

CHANGE BUT FOR THE SAKE OF CHANGE

CANNOT BE A GOOD THING.

TO MORE EASILY ADJUST TO CHANGE,

FIRST ACCEPT THAT YOU MUST CHANGE.

CHANGE IS A NECESSARY PART OF LIFE;

OTHERWISE, ALL LIVING THINGS WOULD DIE.

CHANGE IS VITAL TO OUR GROWTH;

IF WE DON'T CHANGE,

WE DON'T GROW!

INSTANT REPLAY WAS NOT DESIGNED FOR

MISTAKES!

IF WE DON'T LEARN FROM OUR MISTAKES,

THEN WHAT IS TOMORROW GOING TO BE LIKE?

L

O

V

E

IF LOVE IS THE PENCIL,

THEN HATE IS THE ERASER.

JOY CANNOT BE MEASURED

WHEN LOVE ENGULFS THE HEART.

LOVE

TRANSCENDS ALL ELSE IN

LIFE!

LOVE AND HATE CANNOT EXIST

IN THE SAME HEART!

IF LOVE WORKS IN MYSTERIOUS WAYS,

THEN

WHY

IS THE OUTCOME ALWAYS SO OBVIOUS?

LOVE IS A FOUR-LETTER WORD

THAT

HAS

THE

ULTIMATE CONNOTATION!

LOVE AND HATE

HAVE

CONNOTATIONS

AT OPPOSITE ENDS OF THE UNIVERSE!

TO THOSE WHO SAY

THAT LOVE IS BLIND,

I SIMPLY SAY

OPEN YOUR EYES.

IF YOU CAN "TRULY" LOVE

BUT FOR A MOMENT,

YOU CAN LOVE YOUR WHOLE LIFE THROUGH.

IF LOVE CAN TAKE YOU TO HEAVEN,

AND HATE CAN TAKE YOU TO HELL,

THEN WHICH WILL GIVE THE SMOOTHEST RIDE?

H

A

T

E

HOW SAD THAT SO MANY OF US USE THE WORD,

"HATE"—

DON'T YOU JUST "HATE" THAT?

HATE

IS THE VILEST

OF ALL WORDS!

THE WORD "HATE" IS THE EPITOME OF

ABUSE,

MISUSE,

AND OVERUSE.

HATE IS A FOUR-LETTER WORD

THAT

HAS

THE

ULTIMATE CONNOTATION!

YOU CANNOT TRULY LOVE ANYTHING

IF "HATE" OCCUPIES ANY PART OF YOUR HEART!

F

R

I

H E L P

N

D

S

TO HAVE A BELIEF THAT YOU'RE AFRAID

TO SHARE,

IS TO HAVE NO BELIEF AT ALL!

BE DEFINITIVE ABOUT WHAT YOU FEEL;

OTHERWISE, THERE IS NO NEED TO FEEL.

AS EVERY HUMAN HAS A FAULT,

EVERY FACET OF LIFE HAS A BLEMISH.

WHY ARE SO MANY OF US PREOCCUPIED

WITH LOOKING FOR FAULT?

WHAT HAVE WE GAINED WHEN WE FIND FAULT?

WHAT DO WE DO WHEN WE FIND IT?

IS THE SEARCH FOR FAULT EVER

WORTH

IT?

YOU CAN MEASURE A FRIEND'S WORTH BY WHAT

THE FRIEND DOES FOR YOU—

NOT TO YOU!

THE MOST VALUABLE ASSET ANY OF US CAN HAVE

IS A FRIEND.

IF WE WORRY TOO MUCH ABOUT HOW TO FULFILL

OUR LIVES,

THE LIVES WE ARE LIVING WILL GO

UNFULFILLED.

WE ALL WISH TO LEAVE OUR MARK WHEN WE

LEAVE;

JUST MAKE SURE THE MARK IS UNERASABLE.

IF YOU WISH TO NOT BE REMEMBERED,

THEN LIVE YOUR LIFE BY HELPING NO ONE.

DO NOT CHOOSE WHOM YOU WILL HELP;

OTHERWISE, THE TRUE MEANING IS LOST.

DO NOT BE AFRAID TO ASK FOR HELP,

LEST YOU END UP HELPLESS.

DO NOT WAIT TO BE ASKED TO HELP,

FOR THE NEED, LIKELY, MAY HAVE ALREADY

PASSED.

JUDGE YOUR OWN WORTH AS A FRIEND

           ACCORDING TO YOUR DEEDS DONE

WITHOUT CONCERN FOR CONSEQUENCE.

DOING SOMETHING FOR ANOTHER

        FOR THE SAKE OF A REWARD,

IS EXACTLY EQUAL TO NOTHING.

DOING SOMETHING FOR ANOTHER

FOR THE ELATION IT WILL BRING,

IS SOMETHING THAT IS IMMEASURABLE.

THE REWARD YOU GAIN FROM A SIMPLE DEED

SHOULD BE SIMPLY THE PERFORMANCE

OF THE DEED.

TO TURN YOUR BACK ON ONE IN NEED,

IS TO SHOW A SIDE WITHOUT FACE.

NONE OF US HAS THE LUXURY, OR ABILITY,

TO CREATE "OUR" PERFECT PERSON,

SO WHY DO SO MANY PEOPLE TRY?

TO NOT LEND A HAND WHEN IT IS NEEDED,

IS TO MISS AN OPPORTUNITY TO FEEL GOOD!

THE SIMPLE GESTURE OF A HELPING HAND

PROVIDES MORE THAN A HANDFUL OF REWARD.

D
R
E
A
M
S

TO ALLOW YOURSELF TO DREAM

OF WHOM YOU WOULD LIKE TO BE,

IS TO DEPRIVE YOURSELF

OF WHOM YOU COULD BE!

A DREAM IS BUT REALITY

WITHIN OUR MIND!

IN OUR MIND'S "EYE"

EVERYTHING IS 20-20.

LET YOUR DREAMS DO FOR YOU

WHAT TV CANNOT!

TO BE TRULY HEALTHY,

DREAM!

YOU MUST LIVE AND DEAL WITH REALITY,

BUT DO NOT LET YOUR DREAMS DRAW YOU IN.

YOUR DREAMS CAN TAKE YOU

WHERE YOU WANT TO GO,

BUT KNOW THAT YOU MUST ALWAYS

COME BACK.

.

DREAMS PROVIDE US NEEDED SOLITUDE

WHEN REALITY WILL NOT ALLOW IT.

DREAMS ARE THE MECHANISM THAT

PROVIDES US HOPE!

WE SHAPE OUR FUTURE

BY WHAT WE DREAM!

DREAMS ARE OUR PRESENT HOPE

FOR WHAT WE EXPECT OUR FUTURE TO BE.

TO NOT HAVE DREAMS BEYOND THE PRESENT,

IS TO LIVE A LIFE WITH NO TOMORROW.

TO LIVE YOUR LIFE WITHOUT DREAMS,

IS TO LIVE YOUR LIFE WITHOUT MEANING.

H

O

P

E

MAY THE <u>END</u> OF THE RAINBOW

ALWAYS HOLD WHAT YOU ARE LOOKING FOR.

AND MAY YOU ALWAYS HAVE

A PEACEFUL JOURNEY TO THAT <u>END</u>.

TO

    REACH

        FOR

            THE

                STARS

IS JUST THE FIRST STEP IN

                TOUCHING HEAVEN!

HOPE IS BUT A BY-PRODUCT

OF OUR DREAMS!

HOPE IS A FOUR-LETTER WORD

THAT HELPS US PLAN OUR TOMORROWS.

HOPE IS OUR MOTIVATION TO ANXIOUSLY

ANTICIPATE

THE

FUTURE!

HOPE TELLS US WHY WE SHOULD LOOK

FORWARD TO TOMORROW!

TO KEEP BOTH FEET ON THE GROUND,

YOU NEED ONLY GRAVITY.

TO REACH FOR THE STARS,

YOU NEED ONLY IMAGINATION!

HOPE

IS

THE

FUEL

FOR

OUR

INSPIRATION!

C
H
I
L
D
R
E
N

THE NOURISHMENT CHILDREN DEMAND

IS THAT WHICH WILL LET THEM LEARN!

HOW DO WE SET A PATH FOR OUR CHILDREN

TO FOLLOW

WHEN, OFTEN, WE KNOW NOT <u>OUR</u>

DESTINATION.

THE GREATEST JOY,

IN THE SMALLEST PACKAGE,

IS A CHILD.

THE GREATEST CHALLENGE,

IN THE SMALLEST PACKAGE,

IS A CHILD.

THE PLEASURE A CHILD CAN BRING

CAN ONLY BE MEASURED

BY A BOTTOMLESS CUP!

IF CHILDREN REPRESENT OUR TOMORROW,

THEN WHY ARE THEY A CHALLENGE TODAY?

FEEDING OUR CHILDREN THE PESTICIDE

OF HATE

IS WHAT WILL STUNT THEIR GROWTH!!

THE ULTIMATE REWARD IN LIFE

IS TO WATCH A CHILD LEARN.

CHILDREN ARE THE BUDS

    RESULTING FROM OUR SEEDS.

HOW THEY ARE NOURISHED

    DETERMINES HOW THEY WILL BLOSSOM.

WHAT GIVES US THE RIGHT

　　　　　TO STIFLE OUR CHILDREN'S DREAMS

AND TURN TO CONTINUE DOWN OUR OWN

　　　　　UNKNOWN PATH TO TOMORROW?

SHOULD NOT CHILDREN LOOK UP TO US

FOR REASONS OTHER THAN

WE ARE TALLER?

IF YOU THINK THAT WINNING IS EVERYTHING,

YOU'VE NEVER HELPED A CHILD LEARN!

IN THE EYES OF A CHILD, FAILURE IS LIKE

EATING CHOCOLATE AND NOT LIKING IT.

DON'T MAKE IT ANY MORE THAN THAT!

T
O
M
T O D A Y
R
R
O
W

STAND APART FROM THE CROWD

BY RISING ABOVE THE COMMON.

SEARCH ALWAYS FOR THE POSITIVE SIDE

IN <u>EVERY</u> SITUATION

BECAUSE <u>EVERY</u> SITUATION HAS BOTH SIDES.

TO PLAN YOUR TOMORROW

HERE AND NOW

IS TO GIVE YOUR FUTURE A MEANING

THERE AND THEN.

CHALLENGE YOURSELF TO BE BETTER

TODAY THAN YESTERDAY.

A DAY GONE BY

WITH NOTHING LEARNED,

IS A DAY THAT SHOULD

HAVE NEVER BEEN!

TOMORROW IS ANOTHER DAY,

BUT ONLY IF YOU'RE THERE TO SEE IT.

IN THE TIME IT TAKES TO READ THIS,

WE,

EASILY,

COULD BE ON THE OTHER SIDE.

WHILE YOU WORRY ABOUT WHAT TOMORROW

WILL BRING, TODAY,

IN THE MEANTIME,

HAS QUIETLY PASSED.

YOUR TOMORROW CANNOT BE POSITIVE

IF YOU MAKE A NEGATIVE OUT OF TODAY.

PROBLEMS APPEAR WHEN WE DON'T

EXPECT THEM;

BUT IF WE EXPECTED THEM,

WOULD THEY BE PROBLEMS?

AS YOU WAIT FOR WHAT YOU KNOW

WILL

COME,

IS YOUR TIME SPENT

SIMPLY

WAITING?

IF EACH TOMORROW WAS LIKE EACH

YESTERDAY,

THEN WHAT WAS GAINED?

SOME PEOPLE SAY THAT

TROUBLE FOLLOWS THEM—

WELL, MAYBE THEY SHOULD GET

ON ANOTHER ROAD!

IF WE WISHED OUR PROBLEMS

TO BE SOLVED BY OTHERS,

SHOULD NOT THOSE PROBLEMS

BE THEIRS?

IF WE LEARNED NOTHING NEW TODAY,

THEN WHAT GOOD WAS TODAY?

LIVE
    FOR
        YOUR
            TOMORROWS

BUT
    APPRECIATE
            EACH
               TODAY!

IF YOU "AIM" TO BE BETTER TOMORROW

THAN YOU ARE TODAY,

THEN YOU JUST HIT THE BULLSEYE!

THE NEGATIVE SIDE OF LIFE SHOULD BE

RESERVED FOR

THE DAY AFTER WE DIE!

'THO THERE MAY BE TWO SIDES TO

EVERY STORY,

THERE SHOULD ONLY BE ONE SIDE TO LIFE—

THE POSITIVE

THE QUICKEST WAY TO ERASE A FROWN

IS TO STAND ON YOUR HEAD.

THE SIMPLE JOY THAT WILL COME TOMORROW

IS THE FACT THAT TOMORROW WILL COME.

WHAT

JOY

CAN

EXIST

IF A FROWN LIVES IN YOUR HEART?

TO KEEP A FROWN

                    FROM PULLING YOU DOWN,

SIMPLY PLAY A GAME OF HOPSCOTCH.

ALL OF YOUR YESTERDAYS

                    ARE BUT MEMORIES,

SO TREAT THEM ALL

                    WITH PROPER RESPECT!

GIVEN THAT YOU ARE HERE TODAY

SHOULD BE THANKS ENOUGH!

TO

     MAKE

             A

                   POSITIVE

OUT

     OF

          A

              NEGATIVE,

IT ONLY TAKES A VERTICAL LINE.

F
A
I
L
U
R
E

WHAT YOU LEARN FROM HAVING FAILED

SHOULD BE AS VALUABLE

AS WHAT YOU GAIN FROM HAVING SUCCEEDED!

TO CONTINUOUSLY MOVE FORWARD,

YOU MUST,

AT TIMES,

STEP BACKWARD.

NEVER JUDGE ANOTHER BY HIS FAILURE;

IF YOU DO,

<u>YOU</u> JUST FAILED!

TO USE THE EXCUSE THAT YOU MIGHT FAIL,

IS TO FAIL TO ACCEPT THE CHALLENGE.

A FAILURE IS SIMPLY SOMEONE WHO

GOES THROUGH LIFE

AVOIDING EVERY CHALLENGE.

HAVING
          FAILED
                    DOES
                              NOT

LABEL
     YOU
                    A
                         FAILURE.

OUR LIVES ARE JUDGED BY OUR ATTEMPTS—

NOT ATTEMPTS AT WHAT WE <u>CAN</u> DO, BUT

ATTEMPTS AT THE UNKNOWN.

IN ORDER TO IMPROVE,

YOU

MUST

FAIL!

OUR LIVES ARE NOT JUDGED BY A SCORECARD:

SUCCESS—2, FAILURE—1.

IF YOU FAIL AT SOMETHING AND THEN QUIT,

YOU JUST FAILED <u>TWICE</u>!

FAILURE SHOULD HAPPEN BECAUSE OF

HAVING TRIED;

NEVER BECAUSE OF NOT TRYING.

YOU
      CANNOT
              KNOW

WHAT
      YOU
          CANNOT
              DO

              IF YOU WILL NOT TRY!

THE VALUE GAINED FROM HAVING FAILED

AT SOMETHING

SIMPLY CANNOT BE MEASURED.

ACCEPT A FAILURE FOR WHAT IT IS—

SIMPLY REACHING A POINT SHORT OF

A GIVEN GOAL.

AND HAVEN'T WE <u>ALL</u> BEEN THERE?

IF <u>EVERYONE</u> HAS FAILED,

THEN JUSTIFY

CRITICIZING ANOTHER'S FAILURE.

CRITICIZING FAILURE IS LIKE SAYING,

"YOU DIED, BUT DO IT BETTER NEXT TIME!"

AFTER-THOUGHTS

INQUIRING MINDS WANT TO KNOW—

THINGS THEY DON'T NEED TO KNOW.

FOOLS RUSH IN—

BECAUSE SEATING IS LIMITED.

LOVE MAKES THE WORLD GO 'ROUND—

NO WONDER WE'RE ALL SO DIZZY.

STOP THE WORLD—

I'VE GOT A MIGRAINE!

PLAYING WITH FIRE—

WILL ELIMINATE FINGERPRINTS.

A STITCH IN TIME—

WILL SEW UP ANY LOOSE ENDS.

THAT IS EASIER SAID—

THAN WRITTEN.

TOMORROW WILL BE A BRIGHTER DAY—

IF YOU KEEP YOUR HANDS OFF THE

DIMMER SWITCH.

IF YOUR LIFE TAKES A TURN FOR THE WORSE—

USE YOUR TURN SIGNAL.

FOLLOWING THE STRAIGHT AND NARROW—

DOES NOT ALLOW FOR MUCH MANEUVERING.

BITING OFF MORE THAN YOU CAN CHEW—

MEANS STRONG TEETH AND A SMALL MOUTH.

EVERYONE HAS A PRICE—

BUT CAN YOU USE A CREDIT CARD?

DON'T COUNT YOUR CHICKENS—

SELL THEM TO KFC.

IT ISN'T WHAT YOU KNOW—

OTHERWISE, EVERYONE WOULD BE ON

JEOPARDY.

WHAT YOU DON'T KNOW—

IS THE FOUNDATION OF A HAPPY LIFE.

AN OUNCE OF PREVENTION—

SHOULD BE MIXED IN A GLASS OF

TEMPTATION.

HOPE FOR THE BEST—

BECAUSE YOU <u>WILL</u> BE TAKEN.

IF YOU DON'T HELP YOURSELF—

CALL 911.

IF YOU BURN THE CANDLE AT BOTH ENDS—

YOU GET TWICE THE LIGHT.

IT'S BETTER LATE—

THAN SHOWING UP EARLY WITHOUT A KEY.

LOVE IS NEVER HAVING TO SAY—

"GO HOME!"

IF YOU LIVE ON THE EDGE—

YOU'LL NEED A LOT OF BAND-AIDS.

THE EARLY BIRD—

DOES NOT HAVE MANY TARGETS.

HE, WHO PROCRASTINATES,--

SIMPLY SCREWS UP <u>AFTER</u> EVERYONE ELSE.

PROCRASTINATION MEANS—

"NEVER MIND! I'LL TELL YOU TOMORROW."

IF YOU JUMP TO A CONCLUSION—

YOU WILL LAND IN "WHO KNOWS WHAT."

IF YOU PICK UP WHERE YOU LEFT OFF—

YOU, OBVIOUSLY, DIDN'T FINISH.

IF YOU FLY BY THE SEAT OF YOUR PANTS—

YOU HAD BETTER HAVE ON

CLEAN UNDERWEAR.

.

IF YOU SKIRT THE ISSUE,--

YOU SHOULD RECONSIDER YOUR WARDROBE.

IF THE SHOE FITS,--

BE SURE YOUR FEET ARE CLEAN.

IF LOVE IS BLIND,--

THEN MAYBE THE ANSWER IS BRAILLE.

NO PERSON IS A GREAT-ENOUGH ACTOR

TO PLAY GOD.

IF YOU JUDGE PEOPLE BY WHAT YOU SEE,--

THEN YOUR EYES ARE VEILED IN DARKNESS.

IF YOU PREJUDGE A PERSON, YOU HAVE FOREVER

LOST THE CHANCE TO REALLY KNOW

THAT PERSON.

IF ALL YOU SEE ON A RAINY DAY IS WATER,

THEN YOUR OUTLOOK HAS BEEN FOREVER

DAMPENED.

TRY TO SAY ONE THING GOOD, EACH DAY,

ABOUT SOMEONE YOU DISLIKE.

IF YOU BURN YOUR BRIDGES,--

HOW CAN YOU GET TO THE "OTHER SIDE"?

IF YOU RUSH TO CONCLUSIONS,--

THEN GETTING THERE WAS NOT A FUN TRIP.

IMAGINE LIFE WITHOUT A

#2 PENCIL!

"SPENDING" YOUR TIME BEING CRITICAL

OF OTHERS

WILL CAUSE YOU TO GO "BROKE."

A BIRD IN THE HAND WOULD CERTAINLY

KEEP YOU FROM HOLDING ANYTHING ELSE.

IF YOU WAKE UP AND SEE YOURSELF

IN THE MIRROR,

THEN HOW BAD CAN THE DAY BE?

A FINAL THOUGHT (OR 2)

MAY YOU ACCEPT ALL OF LIFE'S REWARDS AND ALL OF LIFE'S DOWNSIDES <u>EQUALLY</u>—YOU MAY THEN LIVE YOUR LIFE IN RELATIVE PEACE AND CONTENTMENT!

MAY THE MEMORIES THAT YOU ESTABLISH TO ALL THOSE YOU WILL LEAVE BEHIND MAKE THEM FOREVER <u>WANT</u> TO REMEMBER YOU FOR ALL THE DAYS OF THEIR LIVES!

ABOUT THE AUTHOR

Ken has spent many of his working years as a manager and/or controller—he has worked in real estate, insurance, and in the manufacturing field. His greatest motivation and sense of reward, though, has been in the field of education. He was a teacher and coach for many years and now operates a county-wide alternative school program for at-risk students. Some of his most fulfilling rewards have come from these young people. He credits his students with contributing to the birth of this book.

Ken has had two other books published. One is an autobiography, and the other is an inspirational/motivational book of prose/poetry compiled by him over the past forty years. (*Inspiration is a Four-Letter Word*). This may be available in the near future.

Printed in the United States
4763